MW01171123

TURNING

POINT

The End of Captivity

Apostle Israel Oyelade

Turning Point: The End of Captivity

Copyright @ 2020 Apostle Israel Oyelade

All rights reserved. This book is protected by the copyright laws of the United States of America. This book may not be copied or reprinted for commercial gain or profit. The use of short quotations or occasional page copying for personal or group study is permitted and encouraged. Permission will be granted upon request. Unless otherwise identified, Scripture quotations are taken from the HOLY BIBLE, KING JAMES VERSION.

ISBN: 9798618330329

For More Information & Invitation:

Email: visionpower2018@gmail.com

Facebook: @Oyelade Shola Apostle

Instagram: @baba_apostle

TABLE OF CONTENTS

"When the **LORD** turned again the captivity of Zion, we were like them that dream. Then was our mouth filled with laughter, and our tongue with singing: then said they among the heathen, The **LORD** hath done great things for them.

The **LORD** hath done great things for us; whereof we are glad.
Turn again our captivity, **O LORD**, as the streams in the south.
They that sow in tears shall reap in joy. He that goeth forth and weepeth, bearing precious seed, shall doubtless come again with rejoicing, bringing his sheaves with him."

Psalm 126:1-6

Introduction

I want you to understand that the above passage is both testimonial and prophetic. Every time you hear or see a sign that says Turning Point, it means you are set up for a turn-around.

The nation of Israel was in captivity in Babylon for 70 years before their deliverance came. Daniel, suddenly discovered in God's Word the plan of Yeshua to bring an end to the captivity of the nation of Israel.

"This whole country will become a desolate wasteland, and these nations will serve the king of Babylon seventy years. But when the seventy years are fulfilled, I will punish the king of Babylon and his nation, the land of the Babylonians, for their guilt," declares the LORD, "and will make it desolate forever." Jeremiah 25:11-12

"This is what the LORD says: "When seventy years are completed for Babylon, I will come to you and fulfill my gracious promise to bring you back to this place." Jeremiah 29:10

Armed with this knowledge Daniel begins to pray. What we find here is the fact that God answers prayer. I want you to know it doesn't matter how long you have been in that horrible situation as you are reading this book now,

I PROPHESY YOU ARE FREE NOW IN THE NAME OF JESUS.

You may be a captive in the hand of the mighty now, but the Almighty is working out your freedom. Because, there is a divine timing for your turn-around. There is a time appointed for your release and it is now.

7

This book offers answers to what captivity is and why many are unable to experience their divine freedom despite several efforts.

Every form of Captivity incapacitates its victims. And thereby builds a wall of resistance against one's purpose and pursuit of vision. This is the reason for massive frustration and increase number of people in depression and anxiety in our communities.

The desire of every captive is to be free. There is a constant cry for a change of situation and Turnaround. But remember that change comes with a responsibility; Hence, Turning Point isn't just a Prayer Point but a Requirement.

This book in your hands is to prophetically lead you into your season of change through divine insights. It's your Turning Point.

Apostle Israel Oyelade

Chapter 1

WHAT IS TURNING POINT?

Turning Point is not a Prayer Point but being Positively Responsive. It's a call to A LIFESTYLE of Responsibilities. You can't experience a Turnaround until you get to your Turning Point.

Turning Point is a place of realization for a need for Change of situation particularly an unpleasant condition. But it is important that you understand that Changes don't take place until there's a changed man in place. And Changes happens by choice and not by chance.

Turning Point is not a request, but a requirement that must be met to command a change. So, it is a time at which a decisive change in a situation occurs, especially one with beneficial results:

A turning point is a time at which an important change takes place which affects the future of a person or thing.

Turning Point is a place of turn around. And whenever a man desires to see a change, he himself must be willing to change. What I have seen in life is that many people claim to have a strong desire to see changes in their lives, business, nation, family and even in their career but make little or no effort to change from their old ways.

Whenever you see a change in a place understand that it is the people there who causes the change. No progress until progressive men are found. If you find a place to be peaceful, it is because peaceful men are in place.

Turning point is a proof of Divinity reaching out to Humanity and it comes as a divine visitation. It introduces one to a new season, phase and new beginning of great and unimaginable things. *Isaiah 43.19 says, "Behold, I will do a new thing; now it shall spring forth; shall ye not know it? I will even make a way in the wilderness, and rivers in the desert."*

The person who has experienced turning point lives in overflowing Blessings continually. Because the

14

presence of God will be made manifest in his/her life.

Obededom is a practical example of a common man who experienced turning point as a result of the divine visitation via the ark of God (Presence of God). When they brought the ark to his place, little did they know that the life of a nobody was about to change, the man who was not valued was about to be recognized by the whole world...

Turning point brings worth and value to the life of a man no matter his state and status.

"He raises the poor from the dust, and lifts the beggar from the dunghill, to set them among princes, and to make them inherit the throne of glory, for the pillars of the Earth are the Lord's, and he hath set the world upon them."
1 Samuel 2:8.

Turning point brings rest on every side *2 Chronicles 20:30, 15:15*. It brings rest on every area of one's life and terminates struggle, battles, disappointment, delay, stagnation, pain, hurt.

Turning point introduces you to a circle of favor. God will give you people in your life who will inspire and help you achieve your goals.

16

You might not even know them directly.

When a man's life turns around for good, it will naturally attract great and influential people. Everything about the person will automatically change for good and that will leave people wondering what the person did.

No man is too small for God's visitation and no situation is too strong for God's intervention. Turning point terminates the old you and reveals a new you people have not seen or not aware of. When you experience a turning point, you naturally become irresistible to miracle and breakthrough. Your life becomes a magnet that attracts testimonies. Esther found Grace & Favor before the king *(Esther 2:17)* because it was the set day for the change of story.

When she appeared before the king and the Bible recorded that he could not resist not making her his queen. Grace & Favor singled a slave girl out and made her a queen in a strange land.

Grace is a distinguisher, it adds Extra to an ordinary man's life and, it repositions the one that was tagged a nobody, moved him from the gate to the palace. Such was the life of Mordecai, a Jewish captive who sat at the gate of the palace of King Ahasuerus. His kingdom reigned from India even unto Ethiopia, over a hundred and seven and twenty provinces.

Turning point brings upliftment and elevation. It moves one from back to the front, it elevates a man from the lowest place to the top, it is a barrier breaker. No man experiences turning point without his level changing. It is capable of moving a man from the pit/prison to the palace. And the Lord will make you the head and not the tail; you shall be above only, and not be beneath. *Deuteronomy 28:13 NKJV*

There are far too many people in this world who go through life carrying a sense of rejection that began in their childhood. Negative words spoken to them in their early years, and oftentimes throughout their entire lives, have kept them down and held them back from being all God intends them to be.

Perhaps you are one of these people. Maybe you've been told you will never amount to anything.

Maybe you were born into poverty, and you've been told you will always be poor. Or maybe you have been ridiculed and told you will never be loved by anyone or will never amount to anything; You must understand that man's opinion can never change God's plan for you.

"For I know the thoughts that I think toward you, says the LORD, thoughts of peace and not of evil, to give you a future and a hope."

Jeremiah 29:11 [NKJV]

For some of us what is possibly hindering our divine favor to experience a turnaround is negative

21

character. Bad character has shattered and scattered the good and great future many desired. While some people loss the opportunity of getting to their turning point as a result of the wrong company they keep. The Bible says, *be not deceived evil communications corrupt good manners. (1 Corinthians 15:33)*

So, what are some of the areas we need to work on?

- Change from the bad attitude that makes you lose favor at all times.
- Change from being disrespectful.

- Turn away from being rebellious to the Authority of the Word of God.

- Turn away from wickedness. Sin sinks and stings.

- Turn away from dishonoring those that God has honored. if you must be honored.

- Change if you noticed that familiarity is the reason why people take your simplicity for granted; no matter the personality involved. And it is important that you also take caution you don't

23

get too familiar with people God brought into your life.

- You may have to change your environment if your Financial Envelope is constantly been emptied.

- Don't let your neighborhood affect your divine relationship with God.

Chapter 2

WHAT IS
CAPTIVITY?

Before I go about defining what captivity means; I want you to understand what brings about captivity in the life of people. The book of *Isaiah 49:24* classifies the sources of captivity into two types.

The first is when a man knowingly or unknowingly walks into captivity. He trades his freedom with either the devil or his agent in exchange for something in return. (it is called the prey of the mighty).

While the second way is to be born into captivity without one's consent. (that is known as a lawful captive, because of an existing covenant long before you are born.)

Isaiah 49:24-26(KJV) *"Shall the prey be taken from the mighty, or the lawful captive delivered? 25 But thus saith the Lord, Even the captives of the mighty shall be taken away, and the prey of* *the terrible shall be delivered: for I will contend with him that contendeth with thee, and I will save thy children. 26 And I will feed them that oppress thee with their own flesh; and they shall be drunken with their own blood, as with sweet wine: and all flesh shall know that I the Lord am thy Saviour and thy Redeemer, the mighty One of Jacob.*

So now, what is captivity? Captivity is the condition of being imprisoned or confined: the state or period of being held, imprisoned or enslaved. Anyone in captivity is subjected to the desires of his master; those incarcerated are not

27

able to fulfill their own dreams. Vision is on hold.

*"Shall **the prey be taken from the mighty, and** shall **the lawful** captive be delivered?" (Isaiah 49:24)*

What is a "prey"? It is an animal that is hunted and killed by another for food; a "prey" is also a person who is easily injured or taken advantage of.

The Pain of Captivity

Captivity is a state of being demobilized as a result of forces of darkness. The inability to fulfill one's destiny, the state of operating below the capacity ordained by the Almighty God, it is the absence of substantive or identifiable progress in the lives of man, the state of being ground to a halt, lack of capacity to excel in well-being, lack of progress in all ramifications, inability to enjoy good health, inability to have a good marriage.

In addition, lack of clear purpose in life, to depend perpetually on the desires of others. To depend on the good-will of others, living on hand-outs, experiencing failure at the edge of breakthrough, etc., etc. These are some of the classical definitions of captivities. The first solution to a problem is to acknowledge that the problem exists. May the Lord open our understanding to see where we have been affected, in the name of Jesus Christ.

Those who are incarcerated lack the capacity to laugh, rejoice or celebrate. Weeping is a constant experience of a man in captivity. But no matter how long you have been weeping; I prophesy, you will cease to weep from now on.

Psalm 30:5b(NKJV) says, Weeping may endure for a night, but [a] joy comes in the morning.

When in captivity, you will experience Shame, Mockery, Helplessness, Rejection & Stagnation in all areas of life. The Word of God reveals to us that Sarah waited in the captivity of barrenness for 25 years to receive the promised Child. And usually in that situation any woman will experience shame and mockery amongst her peers; with a long night of weeping. Joseph's dream became a mirage, backed with rejection from

31

his own brethren; went into captivity, they sold him to slavery.

He found himself in the house of his master Potiphar, (meaning a fat bull. But rather than been bullied he was made a leader amongst others.) Even though he found favor before his master, yet his master's wife set him up. The whole city saw favored Joseph as a rapist who eventually became a prisoner in Egypt. Israel as a nation was in bondage for 430 years. They suffered oppression under their task masters. They were made to serve under severe weather.

In the pain of their captivity they were made not to serve Jehovah.

David, who was anointed, went into captivity of been denied the throne for several years. But one thing happened to them all. Their captivity was turned around. Their sorrow translated into joy. Their struggle became breakthrough and their night blossomed into day. I prophesy a turn-around for you this year in Jesus' Name.

This year is the season of your celebration.

Types of Captivity

There are several forms or types of Captivities, but I will highlight some of them here. And whatever form of captivity you are experiencing right now will come to an end in the name of Jesus Christ.

(a) Captivity of the Mind

A mind in captivity is a mind that is locked up and is a hostage either to the past, situations or powers of darkness. The captured mind is eventually controlled or manipulated into destructive actions or reasoning.

The mind constantly becomes rejective or hostile to the present moment, it becomes the prisoner of the past and will always be restricted.

On Earth, there is nothing great but man and in man, there is nothing great but the MIND. A man who has lost the freedom of thinking right is half dead because the ability to THINK is a man's great distinction. A man who cannot think, is LOST.

Being in captivity or prison of the mind means the person has lost his or her freedom. You must understand that the mind is not an

35

object, it is a process and it is constantly streaming different thoughts either good or bad, positive or negative.

What most believers don't understand is that Satan can step in to imprison the spirit, stealing your capacity to function in the fullness of life. *John 10:10.*

By thought, we create and recreate. What a man thinks determines not just what he says, does and sees, but also what and who he is. The Bible says in *Proverbs 23:7, "As a man thinketh in his heart, so is he."* Your mind and thoughts

36

determine who you are and how far you will go.

When the mind is in prison, it becomes limited. No prisoner in a cage has any right or say of his or her own. Captives live by the rules of their captors.

One of the ways the mind gets captured is when any or unresolved emotional pain is stored, that act is capable of opening one up to be captured by the enemy... When hatred, pain, or unforgiveness is nurtured in the mind, it gives the enemy a legal ground to penetrate and manipulate the mind into thinking negatively. That is why emotional healing is very important through the help of the Holy Spirit.

A mind in captive is a mind void of the love and peace of God. A mind in captivity cannot see or look forward to a better tomorrow, it cannot see or hope for a brighter dawn.

So many people are trapped in fear, depression, anxiety and most times because the mind is already under the influence or controlled by a negative spirit/power, the only solution presented to them by the devil is suicide.

This is why it is so important to constantly renew our mind with the Word of God. But even now, I command your mind healed of any form of negativity.

(b) Captivity of the Soul & Spirit

There is nothing that will destroy your faith and dull your spiritual appetites faster than captivity to sexual lusts.

There are people who feel like the sexual mistakes of their past mean that God would never have any interest in them again-they are too damaged; too far gone.

Their sexual sin has eaten deep into the fabric of their spirit; and so they feel inadequate. Been emotionally unstable, many have ended up in depression and have not been able to forgive themselves.

Sex is not just a physical thing; it is spiritual. The world, sees sex as just for the body as taught in Biology, just like eating a meal or taking a nap. But the Word of God gives us better insight to it. Sex is a covenant.

"Flee from sexual immorality. Every other sin a person commits is outside

the body, but the sexually immoral
person sins against his own body."
1 Corinthians 6:18

The Bible presents sex as a covenant relationship in which the physical body, the spirit and your soul is interconnected. And by way of extension oneness is accompanied in every other area: financial, spiritual, emotionally.

(c) Captivity of the Body

A state of physical or mental suffering: agony, anguish, distress, hurt, misery, pain, torment, torture, woe, wound, and wretchedness.

41

Psalms 22:24 "For he hath not despised nor abhorred the **affliction** *of the* **afflicted***; neither hath he hid his face from him; but when he cried unto him, he heard."*

There are those whose bodies have been afflicted and some are sickly. Sickness is the quality or state of being ill or diseased; while affliction is a state of pain, suffering, distress or agony. But right now, I decree a release of divine healing upon you in any area wherein you are afflicted now in Jesus' Name, Amen.

"Is any sick among you? let him call for the elders of the church; and let them pray over him, anointing him with oil in the name of the Lord: 15 And the prayer of faith shall save the sick, and the Lord shall raise him up; and if he have committed sins, they shall be forgiven him."

James 5:14-16(KJV)

(d) Financial Captivity

Financial Captivity... Is one of the worst kinds of prison a sane human can be found in. It is a hopeless state that gives birth to frustration,

43

disappointment, hatred, failure, depression and the rest.

Financial captivity is a voice silencer. Is a state where you cannot help yourself or anyone else. Financial captivity is a state of financial barrenness, dryness; It reduces one to the dust and leaves them in a beggarly state.

Such was the life of Lazarus as seen in the bible. It is never enough and such a person can never go far no matter how long he begs. The man at the beautiful gate in (Acts 3) is also a good picture of a beggarly man. No one actually achieves or

44

attains greatness living in financial captivity.

Unfortunately, many people even amongst believers find themselves in this state. They struggle to survive, some, the powers of darkness have caged their finances, causing them to labor so much and get little or nothing at the end of the day, from day to day, week to week, month and month and year to year, the story remains same.

I call that fruitless or profitless hard labor and in *Psalms 127:2* there the Bible made it clear that, "It is vain for you to rise up early, To sit

45

up late, To eat the bread of sorrows; For so He gives His beloved sleep".(NKJV) May God give you rest from financial captivity and profitless hard labor in Jesus' Name, Amen.

God's original intention and will for man is that man should be fruitful and prosper in all. There is no limit or restriction to how far you can go or be successful in life for He (Christ) has given us all that pertains to live and godliness. He made man and plants him by the riverside for man to flourish and bear fruits in ALL SEASONS. (Psalms 1:3) Show me a man in captivity and I will show you a man who is always sweating, laboring and toiling on a dry and empty land.

When a man who finds himself in financial captivity suddenly encounters the Game Changer (JESUS) everything about him will change within a twinkle of an eye. No wonder the Bible says in 1 Sam.2.8 - *"He raises the poor from the dust And lifts the beggar from the ash heap, To set them among princes And make them inherit the throne of glory. "For the pillars of the Earth are the LORD's, And He has set the world upon them."*

47

(e)Relationship/Marital Captivity

In John 4, we saw an account of a woman who Jesus met at the well side. *[16] Jesus said to her, "Go, call your husband, and come here." There was an awkward silence, because (For Jews have no dealings with Samaritans.)*

So finally, she says, "Why are you talking to me?" Jesus answered her, "If you knew the gift of God, and who it is that is saying to you, 'Give me a drink,' you would have asked him, and he would have given you living water."

[17] The woman answered him, "I have no husband." Jesus said to her, "You are right in saying, 'I have no husband'; [18] for

you have had five husbands, and the one you now have is not your husband. What you have said is true."

But then, I think, this whole water discussion did make sense… You see, just like this woman daily came to get water, drank it, but then woke up the next morning thirsty again, and has to go back continually to get water, she has gone to the well of romance to satisfy the thirst of her soul. And it would satisfy her temporarily, but ultimately left her thirsty. So, she got out of one marriage and into another.

This time, she thought, she'd found what she was looking for. And again, it worked, but she'd wake up the next morning still feeling thirsty. So, she turned to another. And another. And then she gives up on the institution of marriage altogether. What she does every day with the water pot for her physical thirst she is doing with sex for her soul thirst with different men.

Relationship wise she is a captive until she met Jesus. Maybe your relationship isn't working right now. Maybe you have suffered many heartbreaks; I prophesy, restoration and healing into your life.

There shall be no more disappointment. And for those of you in marriage, God will sustain your homes in Jesus' Name, Amen.

Chapter 3

FREEDOM FROM CAPTIVITY

"He has sent me to proclaim release to the captives and recovery of sight to the blind, to let the oppressed go free..." (Luke 4:18b)

In my ministerial assignment I have discovered by experience that many *"Christians are in Captivity,"*

53

not just because they were not free from the curse of the law when they got saved, but because they lack the understanding of how to exercise their liberty in Christ.

Some of the reasons why some seem to be living in a Babylonian captivity is because they have been taken captive by the world, the flesh and by the devil. But Isaiah 49:25, tells me that there is deliverance and freedom for the captive of the mighty.

"But thus saith the Lord, Even the captives of the mighty shall be taken away, and the prey of the terrible shall be

54

delivered: for I will contend with him that contendeth with thee, and I will save thy children."

A man in captivity cannot deliver himself. This is why I seem not to be in total agreement with the doctrine of man that believes in self-deliverance in the place of warfare. God's concept for the deliverance of a People, Nation, Communities, or family is that he will always send them a deliverer.

Moses was the deliverer for the nation of Israel from Egypt. Joseph became a prime minister in Egypt so

55

as to deliver the people from an impending season of famine.

Also, when Samaria was besieged to the point where women began to eat their babies, even their king could not help until he called out for the Prophet who came to reverse the situation.

Like we see in Psalm 126, it was *"When the LORD…"* stepped in, that Zion became free from their captivity. God's involvement overturns human predicaments.

Hannah was still barren despite her sacrifices at Shiloh, yet without solution. Until God, through the mouth of his prophet Eli pronounced her blessed before the Lord gave her Samuel.

Lazarus was still locked up in the bowels of death. But when the Lord, He's called Adonai, the Ruler of the Universe steps in, and at the sound of His voice, mountains skip like rams, everlasting doors lift up their heads; Lazarus came out from the tomb, Joseph became a Prime Minister, I Prophesy, as you read through this book, I decree that Jehovah will intervene in your situation and turn it around.

This is your Turning Point for a total Turn-around.

The Blessing of Freedom

1. A divine turn-around brings an overwhelming joy beyond description. When it comes, it certainly is like a dream. It is wonderful. ***"We Were Like Them That Dreams…"*** That was their Song. Because those in captivity didn't expect it to happen so soon or they didn't expect it to happen just the way it happened. For them it was a testimony of divine intervention.

   The worst was in view and God

58

gave a turn-around. It was more than they imagined. The children of Israel never imagined that the Red Sea would pathways for their deliverance? When Lazarus died, Mary and Martha didn't dream that their brother would come back to life again.

Your turn-around will be more than wonderful this year. Somebody said something more than wonderful (one-der-ful) may be "2-der-ful or 3-der-ful"!! It will be like you are dreaming! But this particular dream will become so real.

2. **The blessing of Freedom comes with laughter.** The psalmist says, *"Our Mouth Was Filled With Laughter..."*

Hear me, you will laugh and sing new songs in Jesus' Name. If you don't know how to sing just open your mouth and make a joyful noise unto the Lord. Just like Sarah or Hannah, the day their bundle of joy came. I also believe that was the experience of Joseph when he was not only brought out of the prison but the same day brought into the palace!!

The news of your victory will go around. Those who have abandoned you will struggle to associate with you. Those who refuse to identify with you because of your trials will broadcast your breakthrough.

3. The Blessing of Freedom commands Testimonies.

"Then Said They Among the Heathen (Unbelievers)..."

No one covers the glory of the sun; none can resist the moon from shining. I declare to you this year, *"Arise and shine for your light has come and the glory of the Lord has risen upon*

61

you." Even your enemies will give the testimony on your behalf, **"The Lord has done great things for him/her."**

I want you to observe that the only constant in this equation of turn-around however is *"WHEN THE LORD…"* This passage is sandwiched between Psalms 125 and 127. Each opens with God's involvement. Psalm 125:1 — *"They that trust in THE LORD…"* ; Psalm 126: *1- When the LORD…"; Psalm 127:1- "Except the LORD…"*

Beloved, no future is certain without God. He is the only Guarantee if you really desire to make it in life. We are constantly faced with challenges and battles of life that can cripple destinies and shatter the brightest of visions. They are handy in every year.

Your constancy and continuity can only be secured in God and with Him. Money, fame, worldly pursuits cannot help you this year. But as you put your faith and trust in Jesus Christ, you will begin to experience the testimony of turn around for good.

So, will you humbly ask Jesus Christ to be your Lord and Savior now and let Him turn your captivity around?

How to Enjoy Freedom from captivity.

I want you to know that your freedom is non-negotiable. because Christ has paid the full price. But however, you can be denied access to enjoying this freedom if you keep breaking the edge.

One of the pursuits of those following Jesus Christ is freedom;

freedom from negative thoughts and feelings, freedom from sinful habits and freedom from the devil. In the pursuit of freedom such as healing or deliverance, a better marriage or home life with family, and financial freedom, we must remember we must *"seek first his kingdom and his righteousness, and all these things will be given to you as well (Matt 6:33).*

No one is totally free if Christ is not at the center of it all. To be free completely from every form of captivity begins with us discovering the need for a deeper relationship with God through Jesus Christ by

65

seeking out proper personal sanctification which is like having a bath in a spiritual sense. Only then we will be able to stand firm against the enemy of our souls, the devil.

As we consider Freedom in Christ it is important to give some definition to freedom. This freedom captivity is not about political freedom or freedom of speech, but to be free spirit, soul and body.

Biblically speaking I believe there are two aspects of freedom to consider. Firstly, we are free from sin, self and Satan.

Secondly, we are free to become all that God created us to be. We cannot experience the second point fully until we have dealt with the guilt and shame of sin, selfishness and the schemes and strategies of the devil.

How does this freedom happen?

1. God makes us spiritually alive by giving us a new and regenerated heart in Christ.

2. God transforms our heart by his Holy Spirit. Our heart becomes loving towards God and our new family.

3. It sees Jesus Christ as our best friend and desires to love him as the Lord and Savior of our life. By faith, we give our life to Jesus and receive his forgiveness and freedom from sin.

4. We grow in our Freedom in Christ as we engage our free-will towards obedience and righteousness. The end result is we become God's workmanship. We become all that God created us to be.

Chapter 4

THE POWER OF HIS PRESENCE

A man's turning point for a secured destiny begins when you engage God's presence in the journey of life. The Power of His Presence is a requirement for a turnaround.

If you want to experience a turn around you need to come to appreciate the importance of standing in His Presence daily. The secret of success, victory and unusual exploits seen in the life of a child of God lie in the fact that God's presence is always with them.

Do you want to overcome great problems? Do you want to fulfill your divine destiny? You need the power of His presence.

I want you to understand that when we talk about the power of His Presence we are not just talking about *HIS DIVINE PRESENCE,* but the manifestation of His divine glory upon a man's life. This eye-opening chapter will basically show us how we can have God's abiding presence and the innumerable benefits it brings. I pray that you receive the understanding to live by this divine principle if you desire and expect great results!

Exodus 33:13-15: Now therefore, I pray thee, if I have found grace in thy sight, shew me now thy way, that I may know thee, that I may find grace in thy sight: and consider that this nation is thy people. [14] And he said, My presence shall go with thee, and I will give thee rest. [15] And he said unto him, If thy presence go not with me, carry us not up hence.

This was Moses asking God to go on the journey with him. I would like us to pay rapt attention to this insight and hold it securely in your hands and heart throughout this year. Moses did not ask for signs and wonders or miracles; he asked God to show him His way. God answered by saying that His presence shall go with him. Many Christians are completely ignorant of the presence of God.

Having the presence of God with us is worth more than riches or fame or power. We can go anywhere when the presence of God is with us. I can go to many places because His presence is with me. I don't care what direction it is, if the presence of God is there. A sleep is dangerous when the presence of God is absent. In the presence of God, there is fullness of joy but outside of His presence, there is frustration, multiple demons, discouragement sorrow, fear, sickness, sin, suicide, distress, etc. *(PSALM 16: 11)*

The question I would like to ask us is this: Do we have the presence of God with us? Or have we lost His presence? More than anything else this year, ensure that you have His presence with you always. We saw David in Psalm 51:11 prayed what I considered to be a powerful prayer *"Cast me not away from thy presence, and take not thy Holy Spirit from me."* The Psalmist is trying to say that if God wants to take every other thing from him, He can, but God should allow him to always be in His Presence. He says God should not be silent about his matter; even if He wants to discipline him, He can but He

74

should please not remove His Presence from Him.

We need to have the presence of the Lord in our lives; it is a wonderful experience. It is essential in our everyday life. Moses had several problems with the children of Israel; often they would have stoned him to death, then he would remember God's promise: *"My presence shall go with thee and I will give thee rest."*

That is, you can have trouble everywhere, fears, and threats outside. Since you have prayed and you know that the secret of knowing the Lord is being in His presence, nothing will dismay you.

The closer you are to fire, the hotter you are; the farther you move away from fire, the cooler you become. The closer you move to the Lord, the more of His presence you have; the farther you move away from Him, the closer you are to the devil. It is a wonderful thing to be in the presence of the Lord and it is a dangerous thing to be far from Him.

It is a very serious issue and I would advise that you pray Him daily into your life.

(a) Cain Lost God's Presence

Genesis 4:16: "And Cain went out from the presence of the Lord, and dwelt in the land of Nod, on the east of Eden." Genesis 4:13: "And Cain said unto the Lord, My punishment is greater than I can bear."

Cain went out from the presence of the Lord, because he allowed envy to push him out of the place of blessing. Because he killed his brother Abel. It is a great punishment to be out of God's presence.

It is good to pray that you will not undergo this kind of

punishment. Being struck dead by lightning is better than to undergo this kind of punishment. Losing something physical like a leg, hand or even better still an eye is better than losing God's presence.

(b) Adam Lost God's Presence

Genesis 3:8 "And they heard the voice of the Lord God walking in the garden in the cool of the day: and Adam and his wife hid themselves from the presence of the Lord God amongst the trees of the garden."

The Lord God used to go into the garden, in the evenings, to have fellowship with Adam and Eve but

78

when they sinned against Him, they could no longer behold His face.

They had to hide from His presence. They used to live well but sin broke their relationship with God. They were pushed out of the Garden, from the presence of the Lord because they disobeyed God and refused to put the blame where it belonged.

One thing common these days in the midst of Christians is the fact they put blame on others when things go wrong. Beloved, if you go wrong, it is you that you should blame, not the church or your wife or husband or parents, not even the devil should be blamed for your mistakes, but only you.

People say it is the devil that pushed them to do one thing or the other. They forget it is the job of the devil to steal, kill and destroy; he does it effectively when he is given the chance. You are to stay at your own post and do your job well.

When you find yourself in error, repent, cry unto the Lord and repair the relationship between you and Him so that God can re-establish the relationship, and you will be in His Presence again.

Turning Point: The End of Captivity

(c) Jonah Outside God's Presence

Jonah came from the village of Gath Hepher, which was located about three miles north of Nazareth in lower Galilee. But today the village of Gath Hepher is now known as Mashhad.

Jonah was commanded to go to the city of Nineveh to prophesy against it *"for their great wickedness is come up before me,"* but at first, we see that Jonah was scared and proudful. Which causes him to flee from "the presence of the Lord" because he didn't want to go to Nineveh to preach the message of repentance to the people.

Jonah feels that the people are his enemies and he also believes God will repent of his decision to destroy the city. So he went to Jaffa and sailed to Tarshish, which is in the opposite direction.

But the implication of his act of disobedience to God cost him a lot. A serious storm arose against them. And this compelled the crew to cast lots. And found Jonah to be the cause for the troubled waters. In fact, everyone who was in the same ship with him suffered loss.

They lost their goods and almost lost their lives in the storm. And in order to calm the storm, they tossed him overboard, and he was swallowed up by a giant fish (the whale).

For three days and three nights, Jonah lived inside the belly of the fish, where he says a prayer and repented of his own sins. At the end of the third day, the fish releases Jonah onto dry land, where he then travels 500 miles to the City of Nineveh to deliver God's message to the people.

Jonah 1:7 "And they said everyone to his fellow, Come, and let us cast lots, that we may know for whose cause this evil is upon us. So they cast lots, and the lot fell upon Jonah. 8 Then said they unto him, tell us, we pray thee, for whose cause this evil is upon us; What is thine occupation? and whence comest thou? what is thy country? and of what people art thou? 9 And he said unto them, I am an Hebrew; and I fear the Lord, the God of heaven, which hath made the sea and the dry land. 10 Then were the men exceedingly afraid, and said unto him. Why hast thou done this? For the men knew that he fled from the presence of the Lord, because he had told them. 11 Then said they unto him, what shall we do unto thee, that the sea may be calm unto us? for the sea wrought, and was tempestuous. 12 And he said unto them, take me up, and cast me forth into the sea; so shall the sea be calm unto you: for I know that for my sake this great tempest is upon you. 13 Nevertheless the men rowed hard to bring it to the land; but they could not: for the sea wrought, and was tempestuous against them. 14 Wherefore they cried unto the Lord, and said, We beseech thee, O Lord, we beseech thee, let us not perish for this man's life, and lay not upon us innocent blood: for thou, O Lord, hast done as it pleased thee. 15 So they took up Jonah, and cast him forth into the sea: and the sea ceased from her raging. 16

Then the men feared the Lord exceedingly, and offered a sacrifice unto the Lord, and made vows. 17 Now the Lord had prepared a great fish to swallow up Jonah. And Jonah was in the belly of the fish three days and three nights."

All men and women, who had ever made progress in the Lord, had at one time or the other had an encounter with Him. No other thing should be important if you have not seen the Lord.

Groom up your spiritual life and have an encounter with Him. Drop any other thing that will hinder you from seeing the Lord. If you had no encounter with Him, and all that should die are still alive in you, you have not started.

(d) Moses Encountered God's Presence

Moses saw just the backside of God and the glory of God shone upon Him. And when he got back to the camp of the Israelites, they could not behold his face and they had to put a veil on his face.

When you see the Lord and have His presence with you, no demon or witchcraft power can harm you. You need to pray to the point of having an encounter with the Lord so His presence will always be with you.

And it came to pass, when Moses came down from Mount Sinai with the two tablets of testimony in Moses' hand, when he came down from the mount, that Moses did not know that the skin of his face shone while he talked with him. And when

Aaron and all the children of Israel saw Moses, behold, the skin of his face shone; and they were afraid to come near him. And Moses called to them; and Aaron and all the rulers of the congregation returned to him: and Moses talked with them. And afterwards all the children of Israel came near: and he gave them in commandment all that the Lord had spoken with him on Mount Sinai.

And until Moses had finished speaking with them, he put a veil on his face. But when Moses went in before the Lord to speak with him, he took the veil off, until he came out. And he came out, and spoke to the children of Israel what he was commanded. And the children of Israel saw the face of Moses, that the skin of Moses' face shone: and Moses put the veil on his face again, until he went in to speak with him. {*Ex 34:29-35*}

When you see the Lord and you continually stay in His presence, you will not be bothered about the world or what people say about you or do to you. The turning point for Isaiah, Jacob, Moses, etc., happened when they encountered the presence of the Lord and their lives never remained the same.

When you have His presence around you, things will turn around. because no power of darkness can resist His presence. I prophesy. It's your Turning Point, it's your turn around season.

God's presence will not depart from you in Jesus' Name, Amen.

How to Activate God's Divine Presence

The Presence of God eliminates and terminates every form of captivity. There is a complete overthrow. And any power that does not want you to move forward shall be arrested and summarily dealt with. But don't forget like I earlier mentioned that Turning Point is not a request, but a requirement.

Meaning there are things we must do. And so, for us to be able to create an atmosphere of His Presence... We must learn how to tarry in His Presence.

1. Do not joke with your quiet time. - (Psalm 63:1-2)

You must plan to have a quiet time with the Lord daily and regularly, it is the time when you will pray meaningfully, study and memorize the word of God diligently.

The Bible says that Daniel prayed three times a day. You too can. You can, however, choose the very early hours of the morning when everywhere is quiet. You must plan to follow.

You should also decree the Word of God throughout the day from time to time.

2. Do not neglect the fellowship of the saints. (Hebrew 10: 25)

Do not be the Christian who misses services. Do not make this year a year when you only attend church services when there are special programs. Have a consistent attendance of God's fellowship.

3. Always hunger and thirst for God. *Psalm 42:1-7*

Live a clean and yielded life; pursue a lifestyle of holiness *(1 Peter 1:15-17)* and always seek the things of the Lord. God is by your side; there is no distance between you and Him and He is always ready to listen to you and hear your pleas. Worship Him in spirit and in truth; go before Him the way He wants you to.

4. Follow a consistent program of prayer - *(1 The.5:16-18)*

We saw that in the account of the Bible as touching the life of a man called Cornelius -*(Act 10: 1 - 8)*

5. Build intimacy with the Holy Spirit.

Treat Him as a Person reverently, not as a thing. Learn to meet Him and commune with Him every day. *(2 Corinthians. 13:14) (Romans 8:26)* Understand that the Holy is way maker but a Pathfinder. Prayer trust Him to show you His way. *(Psalm 86:11-15) (Psalm 27:11-13)*

When the fire of God's presence is with you, it will melt away every wickedness around you, the way a flame will melt a candle. The little time you spend in His presence, and when His presence is upon you, will clear away every confusion from your mind. No matter how confused and confusing a situation is, the presence of God will bring order into that situation. As Christians, we should carry His fire about anywhere we go.

But one step to sustaining a lasting presence of God beloved, is to ensure you surrender your life to the Lord Jesus.

And in order to do that, I would like that you pray this prayer if you are ready, right there where you are. Say Lord Jesus, I am a sinner and I ask for your forgiveness from all my sins and that you cleanse me from all unrighteousness.

I claim the redemptive power in the blood of Jesus that was shed on the cross at Calvary because of my sins. Jesus, thank you for your Mercy and Love for me; And I promise that

I will never go back to the world anymore in Jesus' Name, Amen.

I congratulate you on this decision you have just taken. I pray that the Lord will uphold you with His right hand of righteousness. He will not allow you to fall, but stand steadfast in His word.

I pray that you will have a personal encounter with the Lord and I assure you that you will never be the same again.

Chapter 5

BOOSTERS OF TURNING POINT

There are several other elements that makes fulfilled destiny possible. I called them Life Boosters.

These elements can be seen as ingredients that make things possible in life. These elements amongst others include: The power of choices, determination, focus, favor, praying and the power of seed, etc. I will be speaking to you on these elements.

(a) The Power of Choice

Deut 30:15-20 I want you to understand that the type of life each of us will have will depend on the choices we make. I believe everyone wants to have a happy life.

The scripture above helps us to realize that if you want lasting happiness (joy) it can only come as a result of making the choice to serve God. There is no doubt sin can provide pleasure and even happiness, but it truly is only for a season.

The Power to make Choices is God's gift to man. This power given to man to make decisions as a free will agent will affect his/her life. The power to choose is very great and we make choices all day and every day. Some of our choices are good ones and some are bad ones. I don't think any of us purposely desire to make bad choices.

To choose is to decide. We choose what to wear, we make choices about what we love to eat and when to eat. We make hundreds or maybe thousands of choices each day. The power to choose is a gift of God and like all power in the hands of man it is subject to abuse.

Therefore, your choice today determines the future you see. Where you are today is a function of yesterday's choices.

Choose wisely because your life depends on it.

(b) The Force of Determination

There is a common saying that, winners don't quit and quitters don't win. Determination is the strength that carries you through the path of success in the midst of obstacles.

The word obstacle is a compound word derived from two words, obstruction and tackle. Every obstruction in life is to be tackled. Demas got discouraged and left the ministry of Paul.

"2 Timothy 4:10 - For Demas hath forsaken me, having loved this present world, and is departed unto Thessalonica; Crescens to Galatia,

Titus unto Dalmatia." Demas was a companion and fellow-laborer of Paul during his first imprisonment at Rome *(Philemon 1:24; Col 4:14).* Paul called him a fellow laborer. It appears, however, that the love of the world afterwards mastered him, and he deserted the apostle *(2 Timothy 4:10).*

There are so many challenges that we face in our lives each day but God has given us the grace and ability to conquer them all. The Bible says: *1 John 4:4* - Ye are of God, little children, and have overcome them:

because greater is he that is in you, than he that is in the world.

John Mark could not stand the heat of the spiritual battle and abandoned Paul and Barnabas in the battlefield *(Acts 12:25, 13:13; 15:36-40)*.

Determination is the strength that carries you through the path of success in the midst of obstacles. The word obstacle is a compound word derived from two words, obstruction and tackle. Every obstruction in life is to be tackled.

Determination is the ability to tackle an obstruction to life. An example is the Tsunami flood disaster. The ocean water came with force and broke through all obstructions on its way because it has a great force.

So, what is the driving force motivating you? For Paul the Apostle, his driving force was the vision he received from the Lord when he had an encounter with him on his way to persecute the believers in Damascus. This is what he said:

Acts 20:24 *"But none of these things move me..."* He said none of these move me because he has a course that is a vision to finish with joy. He

106

was determined to complete the race no matter what it would cost him. The vision God has given to you will not be terminated prematurely. You will fulfill the purpose of God for your life.

(c) The Power of Focus

One major weapon of the devil against God's people is broken focus through distractions.

When your focus is broken, your energy is spent in many directions with no significant achievement.

Distraction is anything that has power (directly or indirectly) to snatch away what is truly yours in life. Whatever can move you from your place in God, is a distraction. Distractions can come in negative or positive form and that is why you have to be careful of any form of distraction.

A focused man does not do trial and error, he sticks to the will of God whether it is convenient or not. He keeps going even when the road is tough. And he never relaxes when the road becomes easy, because of the power of focus. Seasons do not change a man of focus. He is the same in all seasons. Distractions may show up in a negative form, but your ability to recognize them is a major compass to your destiny in life. **PROVERBS 29:18**

Ask yourself, what are the things that are currently challenging your focus? Anything taking your attention from the things of your purpose, vision or dreams, goals or aspirations is a distraction. It can be that little success you have achieved now, which finally takes you from the original reason why you are on the Earth. Beloved, distraction is dangerous, it is of the devil.

For example, a little baby can abandon a bar of gold if you give him toys that look attractive. Don't let the devil distract you from the GOLD of your destiny by giving you toys. Avoid distraction, stay focused on what you know is the purpose of God for you and it shall be well with you in Jesus' name.

(d) The power of favor

Turning point brings you to the realm of unimaginable favor and restoration. 1 Samuel 10:1-

110

Saul was on a mission to look for his father's missing asses but encountered the oil that brought about his turning point. He left his father's house as a man but returned as a king. Not only did he encounter the oil that changed his life and status, the oil made men favor him and gifts were given to him willingly without him asking or working hard for them. Favor will terminate struggle and give you sweetness breakthrough.

When the oil of favor is upon you, men will not need to know you before they go out of their way for you. When Potiphar set his eyes on Joseph, the anointing of favor was activated, a slave boy became a supervisor because he found favor....

When Esther came before the king, the anointing of favor upon her life was activated and it started speaking. The oil of favor activates/brings overflow.

(e) The Power of Prayer

Prayer is one of the most powerful weapons God has given us. Prayer focuses the eyes of a praying individual only to God who is the sovereign Lord. He's the all-powerful God; the One who knows the end from the beginning and who has His great plan of campaign which no-one can hinder.

He is the self-revealing Lord. The seeing Lord God sees all, and waits to intervene and accomplish His will in answer to the prayers of His people. Prayer is the secret of every Believer. If there is a man to pray, there is a God who answers. Someone once said that, to be prayerless is to be powerless. Every time we see the intervention of God on Earth is because some men give themselves over to prayer.

Jabez prayed, Jacob prayed. The bible said that Isaac entreated the Lord for his wife, meaning that he prayed. When she was without a child. Hannah prayed at Shiloh. Those who cannot pray remain prey. If you ever desire a total turnaround commit yourself to prayer.

F.B. Meyer, the author of the great little book, The Secret of Guidance said, *"The great tragedy of life is not unanswered prayer, but un-offered prayer."*

Prayer is the pipeline of communication between God and His people, between God and those who love Him. Many of us have reduced prayer to what we do when there are emergency situations in our lives. Instead of it being something we do every day, like breathing, eating and walking and talking.

it seems to have become like that little glass covered box on the wall that says, "break in case of emergency." It is true that so very often we associate prayer with crises in our life. To live a victorious life; prayer must become a lifestyle.

Today, I can personally say I am what I am by the grace of God through the ministry of prayer. In

Luke 18:1-7, Jesus emphatically declared that, Men ought always to pray and not faint. The Bible also shows us Jesus lived a life of Prayer. "But Jesus Himself would often slip away to the wilderness and pray." - Luke 5:16, AMP

Two of the most instructive parables Jesus ever told on prayer, one in Luke 18 and the other in Luke 11, both have to do with being persistent and not giving up in prayer.

Luke 18:1 says, "Now He was telling them a parable to show them that at all times they ought to pray and not to lose heart."

Luke 11:9 is where we find the promise that says, "ask and it shall be given to you; seek and you shall find; knock and it shall be opened to you."

If you look carefully, you would have noticed that each of those verbs are in the present tense, active voice and could be translated, as "keep on asking, keep on seeking, keep on knocking." Jesus does not want us to give up in prayer, He instructs us to be persistent.

117

(f) The Power of Seed

"*Isaac planted crops in that land and the same year reaped a hundredfold, because the Lord blessed him.*" (Genesis 26:12, NIV)

Genesis 26, reveals to us the account of a man called Isaac who acted by faith to sow seeds in famine. The Bible says there was a great famine in the land.

A drought had occurred for many years, and the people of the land were experiencing scarcity. For them life had become the survival of the fittest. In the midst of this famine,

God told Isaac to take a step of faith to plant his crops.

No one farms in a famine. It didn't make sense. There was no way to water the crops.

In the science of agriculture that looks like a waste of effort, a waste of time and above all, a waste of crops. Isaac with the knowledge of farming could possibly have said,

"God, are You aware of the present situation of the land? The weather conditions do not permit anyone to plant their seeds; because it hasn't been raining in years? Nothing is going to grow."

Isaac could have looked at things in the natural and talked himself right out of it; but instead, Isaac in bold obedience in the midst of the famine, sowed a seed in the land.

And the Bible says that in the same year, in the famine, he received a 100-fold return.

Isaac was not discouraged. I believe folks around him would have tried to talk him out of that faith.

But he didn't listen to the voices of discouragements, he just kept planting. What was he doing? He was sowing a radical seed. What happened? He reaped a radical

120

harvest! If Isaac had refused to sow as commanded in famine, he wouldn't have experienced the turnaround.

Whilst every other person was still living in scarcity, Isaac began to live in abundance.

Noah gave a sacrifice after the flood in Genesis 8:20 after that he built an altar for the Lord. And in verse 21, the Bible says, the Lord smelled a sweet savor, and the Lord said in his heart, I will not again curse the ground any more for man's sake;... But the amazing happened in the next chapter of Genesis in verse one, *"And God blessed Noah and his sons, and said unto them, Be fruitful, and multiply, and replenish the Earth, And the fear of you and the dread of you shall be upon every beast of the earth, and upon every fowl of the air, upon all that moveth upon the Earth, and upon all the fishes of the sea; into your hand are they delivered."*

See what the power of seed could do? Noah was not blessed, but God made all other Earthly creatures fear him. Meaning nothing was permitted to oppress or torment his household.

You also can command God's attention for your turnaround if you can practice the laws of giving and reaping. Genesis 8:22 says, "While the Earth remaineth, seed time and harvest, and cold and heat, and summer and winter, and day and night shall not cease." It is a covenant.

Every covenant practitioner doesn't suffer loss. Order my book titled, *"I hate Poverty"* if you want more understanding on this matter.

Chapter 6
ENGAGING THE WEAPON OF PRAYER FOR YOUR TURNAROUND

Psalm 126:1-3

"When the Lord turned again the captivity of Zion, we were like them that dream. 2 Then was our mouth filled with laughter, and our tongue with singing: then said they

among the heathen, The Lord hath done great things for them. 3 The Lord hath done great things for us; whereof we are glad."

I'll like you to pray these following Prayers in faith and believe God for a total turn around in Jesus' Name, Amen.

Freedom from Captivity

1. I invoke the Blood of the covenant of Jesus to break loose from every form of bewitchment in Jesus' name.

2. I refuse to be a prayer project; I enforce my total freedom from the consequences of every inherited evil covenant

3. I am a partaker of the Lord's Table therefore; I refuse to be a partaker of any bondage from devils in Jesus' name.

4. I engage with my ultimate weapon of blood sprinkling against every Pharaoh resisting my total deliverance in Jesus' Name.

5. By the Blood of Jesus poured into the Earth, (Luke 22:19), I am enforcing my total freedom from all

forms of evil attacks and activities in Jesus' Name

6. I invoke the blood of the New Covenant against all spiritual resistance to my total freedom in Jesus' Name.

7. I use the liberating force in the Blood of my covenant in Christ (Zech 9:11), to enforce my total freedom from all forms of captivity in Jesus' Name.

8. I invoke the blood of Jesus Christ to lose myself from all forms of foundational bondage in Jesus' Name.

9. I declare Death to every Goliath resisting my total deliverance, I command your sudden death in Jesus' Name.

10. By the Blood of my covenant in Christ, I break the power of captivity from every evil dedication over my life in Jesus' Name.

11. I am bought by the blood of Jesus (1 Corinthians 6:10), I release myself from the grip of every spirit husband/wife in Jesus' Name

12. Fire of the Holy Ghost, locate and burn every tree planted to

enforce all forms of bondage in my life in Jesus' Name.

13. Any power, behind the demonic alteration of my divine destiny and virtues, die, in the name of Jesus.

14. Demonic marriage, loose your hold over my life and be purged out of my foundation, in the name of Jesus.

15. Oh Lord! Command your blessing to my life today; Holy Ghost fire destroy every misfortune attached to my name by fire in Jesus' name.

16. Let the fire of God, pursue all strange children and women, assigned to me in the dream, in the name of Jesus.

17. Every evil effect of laying on of hands, lose your hold over my life and be purged out of my foundation, in Jesus' Name.

18. Evil idols from my father's house, fight against idols from my mother's house and destroy yourselves, in Jesus' Name.

19. I invoke the voice of the Blood of Jesus against every Jezebel spirit resisting my prayer breakthrough in Jesus' Name.

20. Angels of God, locate and destroy every item of mine used on evil altars to bewitch me in Jesus' Name.

21. Let the earthquake of God sweep through the covens of witchcraft behind all forms of bondage in my life in Jesus' Name.

22. Jesus Christ has set me free by His shed Blood, I enforce it in Jesus' Name.

23. I enforce my liberty from every family curse by the blood of Jesus.

24. I enforce my freedom from every ancestral strongman opposing my peaceful life in Christ in Jesus' Name.

25. Let every spiritual opposition be turned now to joyful breakthroughs in Jesus' name.

26. Let the force of my total freedom through the blood of Jesus

be expressed in my life now in Jesus' Name.

27. Let the expression of my redemptive freedom appear now in the Name of Jesus Christ. Thank You, Father.

About the Book

Every form of Captivity incapacitates its victims. And thereby builds a wall of resistance against one's purpose and pursuit of vision.

This is the reason for massive frustration and increase number of people in depression and anxiety in our communities.

The desire of every captive is to be free. There is a constant cry for a change of situation and Turnaround. But remember that change comes with a responsibility; Hence, Turning Point isn't just a Prayer Point but a Requirement.

This book in your hands is to prophetically lead you into your season of change through divine insights. It's your Turning Point.

Made in the USA
Columbia, SC
07 March 2020

88851923R00076